Ex Libris

Name ....

Address ....

....

Telephone ....

Fax ....

e-mail ....

ON THE COVER

A Sumerian tablet, inscribed in cuneiform, in around 2300 BCE. Also called the King List. It records the names of the rulers of Sumer.

The spine contains Ashokan inscription in Prakrit language, written in the Brahmi script.

The Akkadian script is taken from a clay tablet of the Middle Babylonian Period.

An iPad

Facing page: A seal from the Indus Valley Civilization, script not deciphered yet.

Text
Hiren Datta

ISBN: 978-93-5036-851-0

Kalabindu Enterprises P. Ltd.
GF–18, Virat Bhawan
Commercial Complex, Mukherjee Nagar
Delhi 110009
Phone: +91-11-47038000

from tablet to tablet

the Journey of written communication

A Notebook

Introduction

One fine morning a government accountant was hard at work. A farm hand had to be paid his dues. He took up his curved reed stem and made wedge-shaped scribbles on a 3.5 inch piece of moist clay—a stick figure with a ration bowl, crescents for days, upright jars for payment in the form of barley and a rising sun between hills to record the time of the day. He then baked the piece in kiln fire, to save it as office memo. Six thousand years later his handiwork surfaced in the course of an excavation in Iraq as a crucial fragment in the history of human communication—the clay tablet, one of the oldest-known mediums of written communication in the world.

That little clay tablet was as essential then as a tablet computer, iPad or laptop is today, on any cabinet secretary's table.

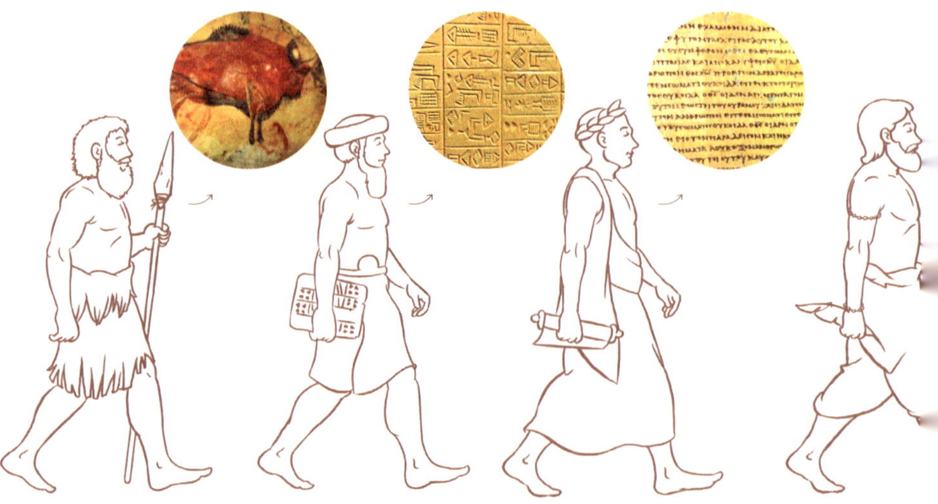

The history of the written word has come full circle—from tablet to tablet. The clay marks have been replaced by computer database. And the ancient accountant has been replaced by applications, which get the database to read and write data on its behalf. It's an exciting journey of discovery—of linguistics, mathematics and above all, human inquiry, imagination and invention.

Without written communication we could hardly have created the human world we know. No wonder the word 'tablet' originates from the ancient Hebrew word *tebhel*, or 'the world.' By 1300, according to the Oxford English Dictionary, the word 'tablet' appeared in English, denoting a stiff sheet for writing on, sometimes several sheets fastened together. It came from the Old French word *tablette*—a table, slab, writing surface or board. Linguists trace it back to the Latin *tabula*. It was in 1984 that the term for anything small, flat and rectangular, came to be used for the ultimate tool of human communication, 'tablet computers,' refined and created in the new millennium as man's best friend—in digital form.

This notebook is a brief ode to that journey.

Actions Speak Louder...

"Mankind stood up first and got smarter later."

— Stephen Jay Gould, Harvard biologist

Two million years ago, as the early morning Sun began to inch up the African skies, a man stepped out of his cave. Suddenly he heard a twig snap. He spun around to find a tiger staring directly at him. "Ahhhhh!" he screamed, reaching down to pick up a rock. He hurled it at the beast. The tiger growled fiercely but backed off. Relieved, the man rushed back to his shadowy lair. He recounted this scary incident to his mates by using arm movements, facial gestures and by making snarling noises to mimic the tiger's roar.

Before speech came body language. Our hunter-gatherer ancestors used gestures, sounds and facial expressions to exchange information and pass down knowledge and wisdom to their progeny.

The evolutionary shifts in the human body transformed communication. Standing upright and walking on two legs meant that early humans could use their hands and upper body for communication using gestures.

As the early human species became anatomically modern, their increased cranial capacity and fully developed neural circuits, along with the tongue, diaphragm and chest muscles led to the use of more complex and distinctive sounds.

But how did meaningful sound develop? According to some experts it came from mimicking animal cries and sounds in the environment. Others claim that language developed from noises linked to emotions and instincts—cries of joy, pain, pleasure or anger, or sounds made to warn each other of danger and the presence of predators.

The need to survive by our hunter-gatherer ancestors gave birth to simple communication such as observing, listening and imitating, using gestures and sounds.

18

Conveyed through Color

> "Painting has been in a state of decadence since the age of caves."
>
> — Joan Miro, Catalan artist

The time is 35,000 years ago. A man is crawling inside a cave. He balances a flickering oil lamp carefully in one hand to light his way. He also carries a little basket with pots of bright colors—red, blue, black, yellow—made from crushed rocks, plants, spittle and fat. He reaches a roomy chamber, puts down his lamp and starts daubing paint on the stone walls.

What is he painting? Much of the imagery, reflected in the light of his lamp, is about a life of hunting and survival—large animals in flight, stick figures of human hunters in pursuit, a pride of lions hunting down oxen, grazing bison and galloping horses. In between he draws triangles, squares, circles, crosses, lines and dots. Before he finishes, he smears paint on both palms and puts them flat against the cave wall, leaving their impression behind—his signature?

These cave paintings are not regarded by modern scholars as art for art's sake. Then why did the early human paint in the recesses of dark caves? Clearly this was a means to record daily experiences, share messages and thoughts and pass on knowledge to future generations. The images may also have been painted to celebrate successful hunting expeditions, or to depict the nature of different animals, or to explain the use of animals for food and clothing. Some experts believe that early cave paintings were the work of spiritual leaders and served a magical purpose—to communicate with the gods and the spirits, or to cast a spell on animals to assist in future hunting.

Through their paintings, our early ancestors recorded the first accounts of human communication. And they also gave us the first set of tools—such as sticks, quills, bone pipes and paints—to communicate with each other.

Hand stencils from Chauvet, France

24

Counting to Cuneiform

" Shamash-Shar-Usur lends 10 shekels of silver to Qurdi-Nergal on security, to be repaid in 6 years. 6 witnesses. "

— Sumer tablet

Over 7000 years ago the hunter-gatherers took to farming and irrigation and settled along river valleys. The earliest known examples of script originated around 3500 BCE in Sumer, the first-known civilization of the world.

Located on the flood plains of the Tigris and Euphrates rivers, in the region that is now modern Iraq, Sumer was a collection of city-states ruled by priest-kings and inhabited by farmers, artisans and merchants. Agriculture and trade prospered. How were trade transactions to be recorded? The ancient Sumerians used small clay objects in abstract shapes, called clay tokens, to keep track of agricultural and manufactured goods. In time, as they needed to keep these tokens safe, they began to seal them in hollow clay containers or envelopes. In order to remember what was inside these sealed containers, the Sumerians impressed pictures of the tokens on the containers. In time, the tokens and envelopes were done away with but the symbols of the tokens continued to be used. Thus the earliest system of writing—the cuneiform was invented. The Sumerian tablets are the earliest examples of the cuneiform script.

Cuneiform was pictographic—the image of the Sun signified the Sun. Later cuneiform writing embraced ideograms. For example, the sign representing a foot was also used to mean 'stand,' 'walk,' 'run,' 'bring' and so on. Much later cuneiform was used phonetically, with symbols representing sounds. With this the journey of written communication moved to its next stage—the alphabet. But that's another story...

The cuneiform script was written on tablets using reed pens called stylus. These clay tablets were then baked in a kiln.

The Writing on the Wall

> "Once you get words and a spoken language, it gets harder to communicate."
>
> — Jane Goodall

The alphabet was not invented by pundits or priests, it was made by uneducated workers. It revealed itself not in royal courts but as everyday graffiti, scratched on rocks and walls.

Atop the high mountains of the Sinai Peninsula in Egypt, from 1900 BCE to 1550 BCE, an area called Serabit el-Khadem was known for its mineral wealth, especially turquoise and the temple of the Goddess Hathor, the deity of the blue stone. As this stone was much in demand among Egyptian royalty, mining became a lucrative occupation, attracting stone-cutters and miners from across the Middle East—from Palestine to Lebanon. They spoke old Hebrew, and found it difficult to pick up Egyptian hieroglyphic, which comprised hundreds of signs. In their effort to communicate, they mixed the two languages and created the first alphabet of the world—the Proto-Sinaitic script.

This strange new script appeared inside mines and within temple grounds. It had less than thirty pictorial signs. Each sign stood for a sound. Vowels, however, were not represented. Thus the pictograph of a house, *bêt* in Hebrew, and drawn as the four walls of a dwelling, was pronounced only by the initial consonant 'b.' Such simple phonetic reading rules meant that ordinary people could at last read the writing on the wall. They wrote devotional messages on the walls, praying for a safe journey home and sought protection for the dangerous work they did. What began as a modest invention out of a need to communicate grew in proportion, with far-reaching social and cultural significance.

The Proto-Sinaitic script spread across the world and had an impact on the growth of Greek and Latin scripts. It became the starting point for all other alphabet systems in the world.

Monuments from Egypt and Ethiopia according to the illustrations made in the years 1842–1845

The First Word

"In the beginning was the Word, and the Word was with God, and the Word was God."

— *The Bible*

Who uttered the first word? Most world religions claim it was God. The Bible says, "And God said, Let there be light: and there was light."

Spoken language is unique to human beings. It is believed that about 100,000 years ago the first modern humans in the African continent learnt to communicate through speech. Later as small splinter groups set off to find new homes, the sounds uttered by them led to the formation of new languages.

At the root of the development of language lay the need for constant exchange of information. Be it to hunt, to farm or to protect themselves from the harsh and hostile environment, humans needed more than signs and symbols to express their needs.

Adaptation and change over thousands of years gave humans a smaller mouth, a flexible tongue and lips that could produce precise sounds. It would not have been possible for humans to speak if the human brain, too, had not evolved around this time and biologically got redesigned to speak. This anatomical combination made it possible for humans to speak. As social structures started becoming more complex, humans needed codified language to form alliances and formulate rules of membership within each group. Language thus grew in complexity.

The ability to articulate abstract ideas and thoughts through complex language has undoubtedly accelerated the dominance of the human species on our planet.

In Egypt the Moon God Thoth, invented the spoken language. And in Islam, Allah provided humans with language. In Hinduism Vak Devi caused all words to come into being.

Ancient Egyptian carvings and hieroglyphic depicting Thoth

Etched in Stone

"If any man, without the knowledge of the owner of a garden, fell a tree in the garden, he shall pay half a mina in money."

— The Code of Hammurabi

As humankind evolved so too did laws to govern the first settled, civilized societies. The Code of Hammurabi is the first written code of laws known to man. It was composed by Hammurabi, the ruler of Babylon, around 1780 BCE. It was inscribed in cuneiform on a stone slab known as a stela. The stelae or stone slabs, generally taller than they were wider, were a favored means of communication in ancient civilizations. They were used to issue laws and decrees for the common people and to record a ruler's exploits.

The most renowned of these slabs is the Rosetta Stone, carved in 196 BCE in Egypt. It is inscribed with the decree passed by a council of priests affirming the reign and ascension of Pharaoh Ptolemy V to godhood. Interestingly, the decree is inscribed on the stone three times in three different scripts. These are Demotic—the native script used by the commoners of Egypt; Greek—the language of administration and Hieroglyphics—used by priests for important or religious documents. Hieroglyphics was a formal writing system that comprised pictorial signs and symbols that expressed not only syllables and words but also sounds.

Soldiers of Napoleon's army campaigning in Egypt discovered the Rosetta Stone in 1799. In 1801 the French capitulated to the British at Alexandria and handed over the Rosetta Stone to them. The deciphering of the hieroglyphics of the Rosetta Stone in the nineteenth century was the magic key that unlocked a treasure trove of knowledge about a splendid civilization.

Since 1802 the British Museum in London has housed the Rosetta Stone, except for the years when it was temporarily moved underground to prevent possible damage in the First World War.

The Rosetta Stone

Papyrus to Paper

> “Necessity... the mother of invention.”
>
> — Plato, *The Republic*

In 105 CE in China, the chief eunuch of the royal court, T'sai Lun, experimented with new materials for writing. He mashed mulberry bark, hemp waste, rags and fishing nets into a wet pulp and then spread it like icing over a screen to dry. The final product was paper—thinner and more flexible than either papyrus or parchment. It could hold ink better, and was more adaptable to methods of large-scale production. The Chinese were the first to use paper and also to turn paper into currency.

Until 3000 BCE ancient humans put their thoughts down on surfaces they found around them—cave walls, bones, shells, stones, metal plates, clay tablets, wooden planks, leaves, bark, ceramic, animal skin and cloth. It was the willowy papyrus plant growing tall in the Nile marshes that changed the history of writing. Pounded into thin, flexible sheets, papyrus became a new medium on which words could be written.

Developed in ancient Greece and made of processed sheepskin, parchment was lustrous and durable, holding ink on both sides. It lent itself best to the codex form of book, where manuscript pages were stitched together, replacing the scrolls and wax tablets of earlier times. The Romans used parchment tablets and small notebooks for writing drafts and notes. Until the 1400s, from the royal courts to the monasteries of medieval Europe, parchment was the standard medium of writing in the West. It took hundreds of years for the secret art of paper-making to spread beyond China to the rest of the world. It reached Baghdad in the eighth century CE, and took another five hundred years to reach Europe. Writing gradually evolved into a refined art form.

In India the use of palm leaf manuscripts, or talapatra, along with the custom of scribes making copies of old texts on them continued as a tradition until the coming of the printing press.

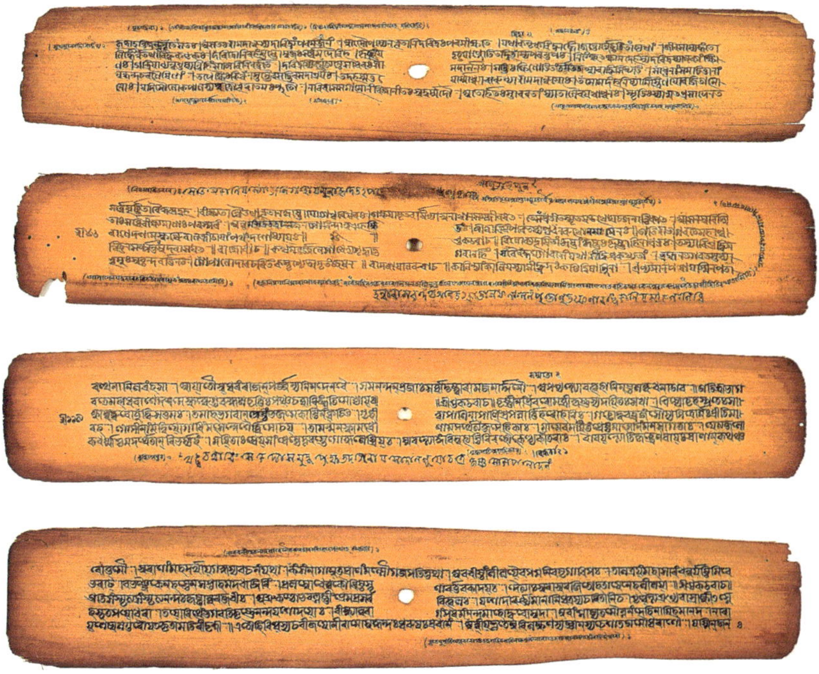

Rise of the Reader

"A book is proof that humans are capable of working magic."

— Carl Sagan

On auspicious days officials of the Mauryan Emperor Ashoka (304–204 BCE), would go around the kingdom and read aloud his messages of *dhamma* to the people. At a time when few knew how to read or write, reading was primarily an oral and group activity. The scripts that developed in the ancient world were hardly reader friendly. The early writing systems did not have capital letters, space between words, vowels or punctuation marks. Both the cuneiform and hieroglyphic writings had hundreds of symbols. Mostly scribes could read and write the languages. It was the Proto-Sinaitic system and its legacy, the twenty-two letters of the Phoenician system, that made reading easier.

In 1000 BCE the Greeks added a great innovation to the alphabet—vowels. The consistent and full spelling afforded by vowels made the Greek alphabet markedly easier to read, even for inexperienced readers. In around 200 BCE came another innovation—punctuation marks, made by Aristophanes, a Greek scholar and chief librarian at the Library of Alexandria. It is, however, believed that the question mark and exclamation mark came from the Romans. Around 700 CE, scribes of Europe invented the lower case. Then came another innovation—space between words.

With these innovations, for the first time, readers were able to read hand-copied books silently. Ancient Roman villas even had private reading rooms for reading aloud in privacy.

It was with the invention of the printing press, in around 1450, that the mass production and consumption of books became possible. The relationship between the reader and the written word was sealed forever.

Greek and Roman scholars copied books by hand in medieval Europe. Only a few thousand books were available during this period.

A Greek scholar hand-copying a book—painting by Raphael

The Printed Word

" And so it is the printing press—the recorder of man's deeds... that we look for strength and assistance... "

— John F. Kennedy

Imagine a dimly lit room, humming with clunky machines, with the scent of chemicals, ink and paper wafting in the air. Strong-limbed men pump machines, load and unload stacks of paper, sort through tons of metal typesets with raised letters, select one at a time from a type tray, line those up on composing sticks, carefully calculate space and text and ink the printing plates—to bring out books that would come out just right. No one knows what Johannes Gensfleisch Gutenberg's printing press looked like, but putting words to paper and sending paper to press took time, tenacity and teamwork.

Gutenberg, a German goldsmith and gem-cutter, is usually credited with inventing printing. In reality, he did not. It was the Chinese who invented printing around 600 CE. The oldest surviving printed book in the world did not come from Gutenberg's press. The *Diamond Sutra* of 868 CE was found in a cave in Dunhuang, China. This Buddhist holy text was printed with Chinese characters on a scroll of greyish-yellow paper, wrapped around a wooden rod. The technique was simple, with words carved on wooden blocks being pressed onto paper.

The world's first book printed with movable metal type was made possible by Gutenberg between 1450 and 1455. It was the illustrated *Bible* in Latin, a set of 200 books, with forty-two lines per page. He perfected a movable type cast in metal that could be evenly spaced and set on a printing press—a revolutionary innovation. The technology made possible mass printing of identical text, that until then was copied by hand or printed from engraved wooden blocks and took hours to complete.

The Gutenberg Bibles, gained fame as the first books ever printed in Europe, and the first Bibles printed in history. Each Bible was complete with beautiful illustrations and vibrant colors.

Art of the Pen

" Handwriting is a difficult geometry and an exacting craft. It is the jewellery fashioned by the hand from the pure gold of intellect. "

— Abu Hayyan al-Tawhidi, Persian calligrapher of the tenth century

The *kitabkhane*, or book atelier, was close to Emperor Akbar's heart, reports the *Akbarnama*, the official chronicle of the reign of Akbar. This is where hundreds of master writers, or *katib*, created the art of beautiful writing with their spilt-nib reed pens, or *qalam*. They created color pigments by grinding metals and minerals—vermilion from cinnabar, green from malachite and used pure gold for illumination. These were then mixed with gum arabic and honey, paper was chosen for its gloss and special ink was prepared that would not smudge the *nastaliq* script that the Mughals favored. Lovingly, they created the beautiful Mughal calligraphic masterpieces.

The Middle Ages saw the blooming of this new form of written communication across the world—China, Japan, Korea, India, Europe and the Middle East. Parts of the *Quran* were initially written on perishable material. Gradually long-lasting and flexible material was used, such as parchment and later paper, bound in the form of the book or codex. The use of sharp and angular scripts gave way to more mature and fluid cursive scripts, making the act of writing swifter.

In China calligraphy evolved over thousands of years and acquired a mystic status synonymous with Confucian culture. In Europe it originated with the Latin script in 600 BCE in Rome. But it was really with the rise of medieval monasticism that cursive script and decorative, illuminated manuscripts got a new lease of life.

The invention of Waterman's flowing fountain pens in 1884 took the wind out of the art and craft of split-nibs and illustrated writing.

Arabic inscriptions in black marble have been used to decorate the Taj Mahal. Most of the text has been taken from the Quran.

Exquisite calligraphy on the walls of the Taj Mahal

Dispatching Messages

“Still on deck with a few people. The last boats have left. We are sinking fast.... The end is near. Maybe this note will...”

— a passenger's message in a bottle, tossed from the torpedoed British ship Lusitania, in 1915, during World War I

Sending and receiving messages have been an integral part of written communication since ancient times. In the entire history of communication, nothing fires up the collective imagination more than the romance of an unopened message in a bottle, cast adrift on the sea. Lost forever or hidden for years, messages in bottles are one of the most archaic forms of communication. Around 310 BCE the Greek philosopher Theophrastus, set sealed bottles adrift to prove that the Mediterranean was formed by the inflowing Atlantic. In the twentieth century, doomed World War I soldiers often used bottles to send their last messages to loved ones.

In the golden years of Mughal rule—under Akbar, Jahangir and Shah Jahan—messages were often sent by carrier pigeons. This was called pigeon post. The origin of pigeon post is attributed to Akbar, under whose patronage the birds were trained and housed in the palace and used exclusively by the royalty to deliver urgent missives over short distances. However, it was not a practice unique to the Mughals.

A trained pigeon's homing instinct made it an intriguing form of airmail for several millennia. By 20 BCE Sumerians had discovered that a trained pigeon could unerringly return to its nest, however far it flew and however long it stayed away. In ancient Greece and Rome, pigeons were used to carry important messages, friendly notes, or state dispatches. A good carrier pigeon could fly 50–90 miles in an hour. Pigeons were used as messengers even as late as the Franco-Prussian War in 1870.

In the sixteenth century, the English navy used bottles to send ashore information on enemy positions. These days drift bottles are used by oceanographers to study global currents.

Message in a bottle on a beach

Coded Communication

" What hath God wrought? **"**

— Samuel Finley Breese Morse's first telegraphic message

Across civilizations and through time, the science of veiled writing—based on linguistics, mathematics, symbols, common sense and logic—created a range of communication systems. Secret codes and the need to break them have had a dramatic impact on history.

The Roman Emperor Julius Caesar was a master of cryptography. He used a simple algorithm, some 2000 years ago, to communicate with his army. It is now known as the 'Caesar Cipher.' Each letter of a message was shifted to a fixed distance—two to the right, so that A became C and B became D and so on. Going by this code, 'Caesar' would read as 'Ecguct.'

As we continue on our journey to trace man's endeavor to make the technology of communication more sophisticated, the contribution of Samuel Finley Breese Morse comes to mind. Morse patented a working telegraph machine in 1837. It sent electrical signals over long distances through wires, and used a code of dots, dashes and spaces corresponding to the alphabet and numbers, later known as the Morse Code. The introduction of the telegraph thus brought about a revolution in long-distance communication. It was used in the two World Wars to send and receive messages. This technology was also used all over the world to send telegrams. Our nation bade farewell to the 163-year-old Indian telegram service on July 14, 2013, marking the end of an era.

The story of coded communication will be incomplete without the mention of Braille, invented by Louis Braille (1809–1852). It is a writing system that enables visually challenged and partially sighted people to read and write through touch.

Today Braille users can read books, menus, signs, currencies, elevator buttons, computer screens and other electronic devices.

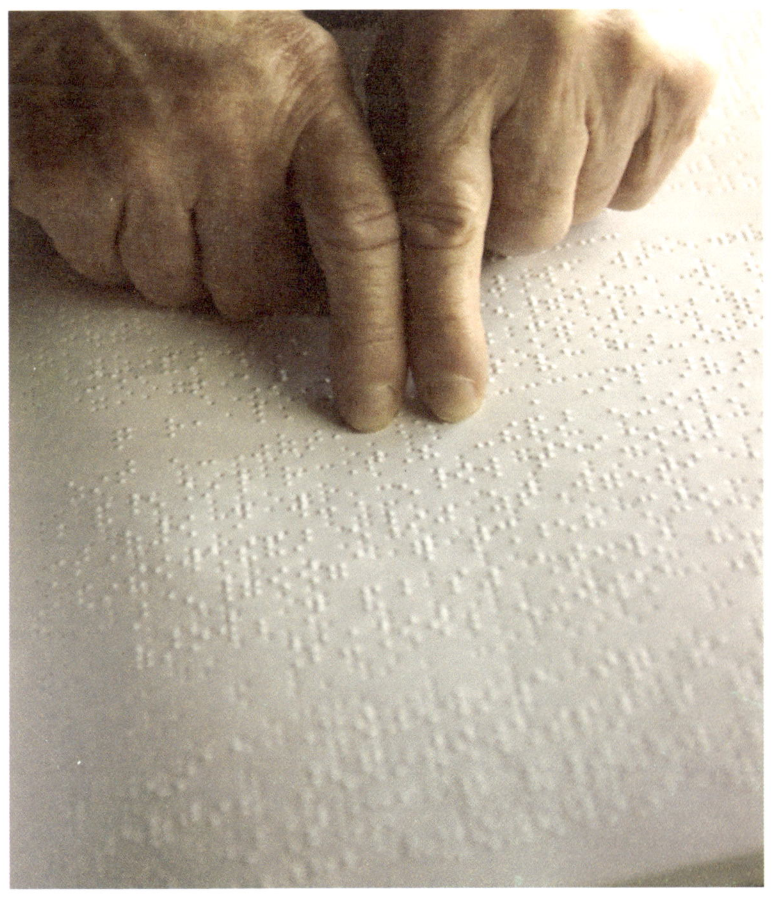

Keys and Bits

“ The great thing about a computer notebook is that no matter how much you stuff into it, it doesn't get bigger or heavier. ”

— Bill Gates

Toward the end of the nineteenth century people started using typewriters. Christopher Sholes, an American mechanical engineer invented the first practical modern typewriter in 1866, with technical and financial support from his business partners Samuel Soule and Carlos Glidden. This typewriter had a type-bar system and the universal keyboard was the machine's novelty. However, the keys jammed easily. To solve this problem, a business associate, James Densmore, suggested splitting up keys for letters commonly used together. This became today's standard 'QWERTY' keyboard. James Densmore convinced E. Remington and Sons, the famous rifle manufacturers, to market the device. Improvements made by Remington engineers gave the typewriter machine its market appeal and sales skyrocketed.

Typewriters were replaced by personal computers and home printers around the middle of the twentieth century. Information was starting to get digitized and computed upon. In 1946 the ENIAC computer, one of the first electronic, reprogrammable, general-purpose computers, was developed. Personal computers gave people the liberty to organize data before printing it on paper.

With more powerful computers being introduced, voice recognition software was introduced. With appropriate software, one can now 'write' a report by dictating it, without even lifting a finger! Now ePaper displays have also been invented. Their use has led to the revolution of eReaders and eBooks because they make it easy to read long texts and smaller batteries make them portable.

Mobile electronic devices called eBook readers are popularly used to read eBooks and periodicals these days.

New Age Printing

"Before printing was discovered,
a century was equal to a thousand years."

— Henry David Thoreau

From the time Gutenberg set up his press in Germany, the speed with which printing presses and their operators fanned out across Europe and the rest of the world is extraordinary.

In the twentieth century technology made great progress and the printing presses, too, evolved. The monotype and the letterpresses became a part of history and their parts became collectors' items. Offset technology is the most popular printing technology that is used in recent times. This involves making positives or negatives, as is done in film cameras, from page layouts. These are used to make plates which when installed on the printing press, make the final impression on paper.

Offset technology uses tiny droplets of ink. These are visible with magnifying glasses on most printed material. Multiple colors, apart from black, are achieved by mixing dots of cyan, magenta and yellow and a separate plate is used for each color.

As computers became commonplace, one of their first uses was in desktop publishing, making layout and designing very easy. Gradually, intermediate steps in printing started getting eliminated. The positives and negatives gave way to the direct development of plates.

Lately desktop printer technologies have matured for commercial use. Digital printing is now being done by using laser and inkjet technology. Inkjet is now being used for commercial printing, eliminating plates altogether. When an order is received, it is possible to print customized versions of a book or document—where each printed copy is different from the other. This is called Print on Demand (POD).

Print on Demand allows books, posters, folders, catalogues, calendars, mailers and other items to be printed only when a customer orders it.

114

Bits Going Places

"Don't use big words, they mean so little."

— Oscar Wilde

While computers were buzzing along and evolving, we were also trying to transmit those very bits of data over long distances. In 1974 the Internet Protocol or IP in short, one of the very basic languages that two devices could use to communicate, was invented. So now we didn't really have to print our letters and stories and ship stuff around! We could send emails.

The World Wide Web, developed in 1989, allowed people to put up information on a server and let the whole world read it. Mobiles and wireless technology allowed us to do all this outdoors! New technology to share information made a significant impact on our lives.

SMS: Emails r now passe. Nw we hv txt msgs. Gr8 4 sharing small bits of info. Wht's the wrld cumin 2?

Social Networking Sites: Facebook allows us to find our friends and to establish a link with them. Here we can share the day-to-day events of our lives as they happen. We can also chat with our friends.

Twitter: Writing on webpages was clumsy. Facebook did not allow easy readability on phones. The information had to be byte sized. Thus came along twitter. U share byte sized msgs called 'tweets.' #Tweeple who are interested in you, follow u & read wht u hv 2 say. Pls RT.

In recent times the hardware, the keys, the screen, as well as the technology to communicate have integrated into a compact device that can fit in our hands. Before we realized it, buttons and keys became old fashioned! We are now in the touchscreen age—we now have smartphones, tablets and even phablets!

The overall variety of devices has allowed for newer ways for us to share information. We have come a long way from etching words on stone tablets to tapping messages on digital tablets.

ACKNOWLEDGEMENTS

PHOTO CREDITS

Pages 2-3	Eduardo Rivero/Shutterstock.com
Page 5	Wikimedia Commons
Page 6 (left)	Rameessos/Wikimedia Commons
Page 6 (center)	Wikimedia Commons
Page 6 (right)	Wikimedia Commons
Pages 6-7 (center)	Wikimedia Commons
Page 7 (left)	Wikimedia Commons
Page 7 (center)	Menna/Wikimedia Commons
Page 7 (right)	Audrey Popov/Shutterstock.com
Page 14 (left)	Locutus Borg/Wikimedia Commons
Page 14 (right)	I. Pilon/Shutterstock.com
Page 15	Victor M. Vasnetsov/Wikimedia Commons
Page 22	Siloto/Shutterstock.com
Page 23	Eduardo Rivero/Shutterstock.com
Page 31	Wikimedia Commons
Page 38	Brooklyn Museum/Wikimedia Commons
Page 39	Wikimedia Commons
Page 46	Vladis Chem/Shutterstock.com
Page 47	Macfuton/Shutterstock.com
Page 54	Sculpture by Thomas Jones/Wikimedia Commons
Page 55	Olaf Herrmann/Wikimedia Commons
Page 64	Nimon/Shutterstock.com
Page 65	Olaf Herrmann/Wikimedia Commons
Page 70	Atovot/Shutterstock.com
Page 71	Wikimedia Commons
Page 79	Everett Historical/Shutterstock.com
Page 86	Garsya/Shutterstock.com
Page 87	3000AD/Shutterstock.com
Page 92	Joao Virissimo/Shutterstock.com
Page 93	Shaiith/Shutterstock.com
Page 98	Villorejo/Shutterstock.com
Page 99	Vasileios Karafillidis/Shutterstock.com
Page 104	Arunas Gabalis/Shutterstock.com
Page 110	Gilmashin/Shutterstock.com
Page 116	Niroworld/Shutterstock.com
Page 117	Eduardo Rivero/Shutterstock.com
Endpaper	Eduardo Rivero/Shutterstock.com

Don't just read about written communication.

Go on, pick up your pen, and fill this notebook up with your ideas. You want to share them? Pick your preferred medium(s) of written communication and send them to your friends and us too:

SMS: send an SMS to 9870845678: Type RSTAB <write your thoughts here>

Email: feedback@ratnasagar.com

Postal Address:
Tablet Notebook
Ratna Sagar Pvt. Ltd.
Virat Bhavan, Commercial Complex
Mukherjee Nagar
Delhi 110009
(*So you like the smell, touch and convenience of paper!*)

Facebook: please visit rsgr.in/ntblt and click

Twitter: tweet to us on @ratnasagarwords

Telepathy: *Under Construction. Sorry for the Inconvenience.*

Oh, and one last thing, spread the written word. You can choose to use a photocopier and share stories from this notebook with friends, students and others. Or better still, if you have one very *special person* you want to share this with, send us the name and address of that person and we will send her/him this Notebook.